MYSTICAL

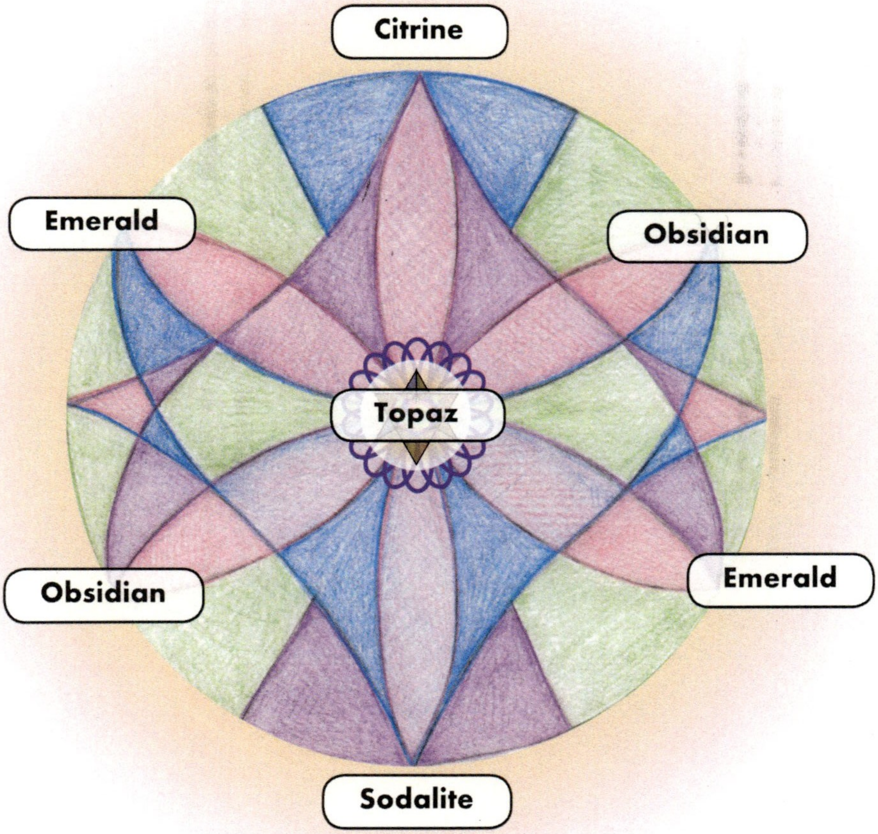

- Citrine
- Emerald
- Obsidian
- Topaz
- Obsidian
- Emerald
- Sodalite

MYSTICAL POWER GRID

The Mystical Power Grid is a crystal grid designed to help you adore and utilize your mystical gifts. Just by having this grid and its beautiful design in your possession, you stimulate the trust of your psychic senses. By adding the specified crystals in their labeled spots, you magnify the power of this grid ten-fold. These crystals are easy to acquire. For the specified crystal type, the size and color is based on your preference.

To energize this grid further, please state: "I place myself in this grid for inspired healing."

The Mystical Power Grid is one of 80 grids that can be found in the book: **Divine Grids: Celebration of Crystal Healing**, or in the abridged edition, **Divine Grids: a Focus on the Crystal Grids.** Each grid was channelled into Rebecca Cohen, founder of The Path to Heal from the Goddess ISIS. ISIS's energy is unconditional love, directing humanity to discover complete acceptance of self, leading to the complete acceptance of others, resulting in peace in your bodies and peace on earth. These grids are part of The Path to Heal.

Thanks for visiting us!

www.thepathtoheal.com

 The Path to Heal

 thepathtoheal

Rebecca Cohen
Founder of The Path to Heal

Email: info@thepathtoheal.com
610-357-0377

Meditate With Your Angels

A Companion Book to The Embraced
By Your Angels Card Deck

©Rebecca Cohen, May 2019

TABLE OF CONTENTS

Introduction 4
Exercises and Meditation 4
Family Fundamentalism 5
Messages from your Angels 7
Adriel 8
Arariel 9
Ariel 10
Azrael 11
Barachiel 12
Cassiel 13
Chamuel 14
Cherub 15
Daniel 16
Eremiel 17
Gabriel 18
Hadraniel 19
Hahasiah 20
Haniel 21
Hashmal 22
Helet 23
Imamiah 24
Jarahmeel 25
Jehudiel 26
Jophiel 27
Kerubiel 28
Laileh 29
Metatron 30
Michael 31
Muriel 32
Netzach 33
Nithael 34
Nuriel 35
Peniel 36
Raguel 37
Raphael 38
Raziel 39
Remiel 40
Rikbiel 41
Sachiel 42

Salaphiel	43
Sandalphon	44
Sarah	45
Seraphina	46
Uriel	47
Vehuel	49
Zadkiel	50
Zaphkiel	51

Path Practitioner Protocols 52
Protocol: Perfectly Imperfect 52
Protocol: Family Love 53
Protocol: Sacred Truths 54
Protocol: I Shine 55

Card Spreads 56
I Fill My Life with Peace 57
Conflict Resolution 58
Chronic Illness 59

Introduction

Meditate With Your Angels contains the same angelic messengers as the **Embraced by Your Angels Card Deck**[1] – however both the book and deck can also be used as stand-alone products.

The loving energy of the angels are the many faces of God. When differing energies are needed to bolster us, the best angelic messenger answers our prayers. Most of the angels in this book are mentioned in a biblical source. However, the sources can conflict with each other about the role of the angel. Therefore while creating the deck and book, I channeled the most important message that the angel wanted to share. The angels presented themselves to me as both genderless and formless. Therefore I use symbols to represent them.

The message from the card deck appears on top of each page. Further messaging is then presented in the book.

Exercises and Meditation

Each angel shared with me how best to connect with their energy to receive directed help through a specific meditation or exercise. These exercises help us release pain points (physical pain, fear, shame, guilt) through connecting to the love that is always there. It can be difficult to release our pain and shame without the presence of absolute divine love, and that's why we call the angels in.

Through these meditations, we release our pain, immediately feeling lighter and brighter. It then becomes easy for us to define our empowered path, creating joy and fulfillment for all.

---

[1] Deck can be purchased on www.thepathtoheal.com

To do these meditations, read what the angel has to share and slowly follow the defined steps. Often the message says "enter into a meditative state." You can do this by taking deep breaths or by stating a mantra or any other way you use to still your mind.

If you are guiding someone else through these meditations, read the steps slowly and feel free to expand on the steps based on what you as the guide are hearing or feeling.

Essential oils are often used to initiate the meditation and to intensify the angelic connection.[2] Sometimes crystals are recommended as well. To learn more about crystals and essential oils, feel free to refer to Rebecca Cohen's books: **Plant Medicine** and **Crystal Medicine**.

Some of the meditations recommend opening a crystal grid from the book **Divine Grids, a Celebration of Crystal Healing**, by Rebecca Cohen. If this cannot be done, then ask to be energetically placed within the grid. The grids included within are: Miracle of Me, Transcendence, Beauty and Living My Bliss.

Family Fundamentalism

These meditations help us heal a phrase that I coined: "family fundamentalism." Family fundamentalism refers to "truths" that loved ones hold that are not based in love. Families stick to their fundamentalism because families believe that these "truths" are core to the family's well-being. Examples are: food is an evil temptress; don't let others see your weaknesses or imperfections (aka don't forgive); we are defective because we've been given the short end of the stick. The fundamentalism takes hold to the extent that we believe that the lack of adherence to these perceived truths might cause the family to cease to exist. These "truths" have often been handed down from our

---

[2] If you would like guidance as to where to purchase these oils, please go to www.thepathtoheal.com.

ancestors for generations and are coded into our genes. Disregarding family fundamentalism creates shame for family members. Considering the possibility of moving beyond the fundamentalism and releasing the shame causes panic.

The shift that is taking place in the world to a more loving energy is causing wide-spread panic to our youth because of the unconscious fear of disrupting family fundamentalism. **The Path to Heal** system utilizes the loving energy of our angels help disconnect us from family fundamentalism. Angelic love releases the shame and panic by providing the knowingness that embracing our personal truth of compassion and self-love not only heals all, but creates empowerment and bliss.

Messages from your Angels

An Angel in Each Direction: When I feel fear, I see the angels that surround me and they show me that all is well and that my life is always beautiful. I am safe.

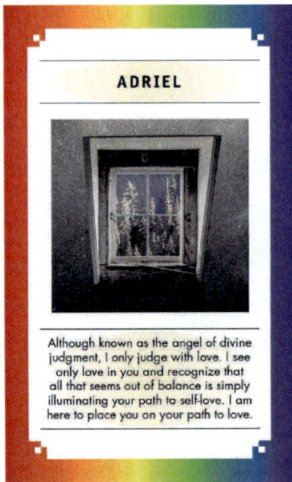

Adriel

Although known as the angel of divine judgment, I only judge with love. I see only love in you and recognize that all that seems out of balance is simply illuminating your path to self-love. I am here to place you on your path to love.

As the angel of divine judgment, I release you self-judgment and replace it with divinity. I help you identify, examine, then heal your shame and blame. The healing occurs when self-love replaces shame and blame. Once healed the magic happens. Physical symptoms and emotional conditions dissipate and miracle healing may result. (**The Path to Heal** sessions will do this too!)

To work with me, diffuse wild orange then breathe it in for a few moments. Go into a meditative state while asking me to illuminate your areas of darkness. After a few breaths, negative images will dissipate. You will then see hearts (or other symbols of love) where there were none. Allow yourself to relax into this love. All is healed.

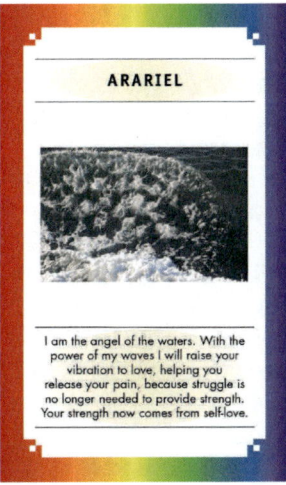

Arariel

I am the angel of the waters. With the power of my waves I will raise your vibration to love, helping you release your pain, because struggle is no longer needed to provide strength. Your strength now comes from self-love.

As the angel of the waters, I give you comfort. It is the human condition to feel out of place and somehow not right. This perception of separateness from others is not found in water, as all is oneness and flow. Therefore I have the ability to help you feel at one with the whole. When oneness is felt, there is only love, and therefore struggle is released.

Meditating with me works best in water. Meditate with me in the shower, bath, river, lake or ocean. Relax with the water and affirm, "I am one with all, I am always at home." When my magic happens you will know oneness, and you will discover that you do belong, always.

Ariel

I bring your divine plan to you so that you know where you are and where to go. I will open doors for you. Your only job is to go through them.

I am the lion of God. Because the lion is at the top of the food chain I am able to understand the intricacies of the natural world. Connecting with me makes it easier for you to succeed in and feel connected to the natural world. With my help you can understand your path fully and seize upon opportunities as they present themselves.

To work with me, I ask that you diffuse clove then breathe it in for a few minutes. I then ask you to visualize yourself resting in a natural setting that is a source of comfort to you. Once rested, I ask you to stand up and look for a well-lit path. Travel that path and see where it takes you. Go through doors as they present themselves. Discover what's on the other side. You dreams are waiting for you.

Azrael

I will help you find comfort in transitions and guide you to discover peace and bliss in times of change.

I am the angel of transitions. Transitions can be very complicated because to succeed we need to depend on our own truths rather than family fundamentalism (see Introduction for definition). Breaking from familial "truths" that are not based in love causes shame and panic. I will help you release your fear, so that transitions yield smooth and abundant success.

To work with me, diffuse geranium essential oil and breathe it in for a few minutes. Then enter into a meditative state, allowing your unconscious to surface a pain point from childhood (often a time when you were labeled the bad one). I will send you words and images to help you see that this was a moment in which your loving truth was in conflict with a familial "truth". I will pour love into this wound, allowing it to heal so that you can now own your own truth. Flowing with change is now easy!

Barachiel

I bless and protect you as you discover that absolute bliss is absolute truth.

I am the angel of blessings. I deliver blessings to you, first in the form of helping you understand your personal truths, and then by helping you live your truth to create your blessed life.

To work with me diffuse rosemary essential oil then breathe it in for a few minutes. Then close your eyes and take five deep breaths. Ask me questions regarding your internal and external conflicts so that I can help you discern your truths. When you are at peace with your truths, you will walk your sacred path with your head held high and it will be easy to create the blessings that are yours to have.

Note: The Living My Bliss Grid from **Divine Grids a Celebration of Crystal Healing** *by Rebecca Cohen is energetically opened to support this meditation and healing. If you have the book, it is recommended to build the grid and have it present during this meditation.*

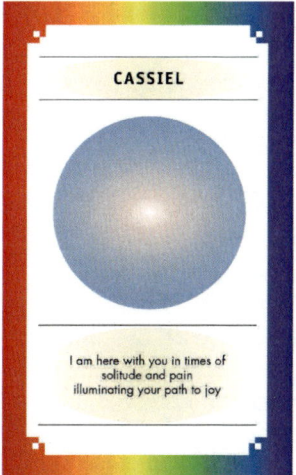

Cassiel

I am here with you in times of solitude and pain illuminating your path to joy.

I am the angel that lifts the heavy heart. When anger, rage, jealousy and grief take hold, I am the angel that helps you release the despair while connecting to the loving energies that surround you so that you rediscover joy.

To work with me, diffuse geranium then breathe it in for a few minutes. Please enter a meditative state. I ask that you open up your pain points and share them with me. For each pain point, I will illuminate the loving answers that will resolve the pain. During meditation follow the well-lit path and allow joy to infuse into you during the journey. In time, the pain points will resolve and what is left is happiness. The journey is worth it.

Chamuel

I bring you peace by helping you see your beauty, and by helping you exist in the only lasting emotion there is, which is love.

I am the angel of spiritual awakening. I help you see that love and God are one in the same. There is no God where there is no love. When you discover love, you can see yourself as God sees you, a beautiful person who is here to help others grow into peaceful, accepting and beautiful people.

To work with me, sniff rose essential oil[3]. Enter a meditative state and ask me to help you experience God. This experience will bring you into a state where there is no other emotion other than love. This feeling of love allows you to experience everything around you (including yourself) as peaceful, perfect and beautiful. In this state, you will know your purpose and you will move forward without hesitation because it feels so good. As you awakening, you will gladly bring others with you. In time, the world heals as you lead the way.

---

[3] Rose is a very expensive oil. It is less expensive to buy a Rose Hydrolot (which is produced from the water runoff when harvesting rose oil), or use rose mixed with fractionated coconut oil.

Cherub

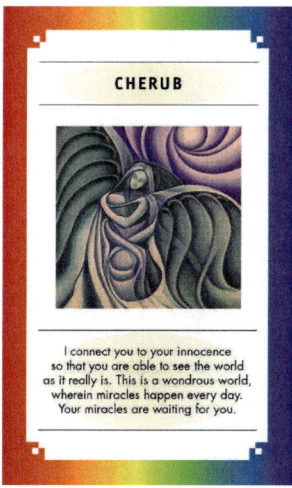

I connect you to your innocence so that you are able to see the world as it really is. This is a wondrous world, wherein miracles happen every day. Your miracles are waiting for you.

I represent all the angels that serve both God and humanity. My job is to help you release your perceived role of judge and jury. Once released, you discover your new role of lover of life. When judgment stops, a miraculous life begins.

Before working with me, write a list of all the ways that you judge yourself. Read the items on the list to me. You will find that in my presence the items are difficult to read because they are perception, not truth. In my presence only truth can be felt. So as you slowly read the items, I will remove the false perception and remind you that you are simply being unkind to yourself in order to box yourself into behavior that you believe keeps you safe from criticism. I will help you see the truth, which is that you are talented, kind and powerful. Work with me until you believe the truth and then your wondrous life takes hold.

Daniel

When all seems impossible, I will help you discover what is not only possible, but what is brilliant and beautiful.

I am the angel of optimism. In an enlightened state, you never doubt your internal compass and therefore your life is a synchronistic miracle. The life that most humans live is so filled with doubt, guilt and shame that you disconnect from your compass. Your disconnection makes manifestation difficult and pessimism sets in. I will reconnect you to your heart-based guidance system so that your brilliant and beautiful life easily manifests.

To work with me diffuse peppermint then breathe it in. Then enter a meditative state. Proceed by asking me a question such as "why don't I like my job." I will then reconnect your knowingness to your heart and you will receive the answers that you are looking for. I will stay with you beyond your meditation so that you stay connected to your heart as you allow your decisions to always be accessible and easy. The result is that you discover the natural ways to manifest an easy life.

Eremiel

I watch over you in times of struggle as I help you find the courage and faith to fully shine your powerful light onto your loved ones and the planet. Your life is a miracle.

I am the angel of **The Path to Heal**. I am here to give you the faith that when you fully accept yourself, your triggers disappear. My energy helps you release the pressure that you put on yourself and others. This pressure creates intense drama. By releasing the pressure, you release the drama. Then it's easy to shine.

To work with me, I ask that you hold a piece of selenite. Selenite helps you cut cords to the drama. I will help you recognize that the drama exists so that you have someone to blame that isn't yourself. I will also help you recognize that what you really feel is guilt. When asking for my help during meditation, I will help you discover where your guilt lies. Once we identify this, you will no longer unconsciously create situations to create a pretense of feeling better about yourself. Instead, you will simply release the guilt. When the triggering drama disappears, your power intensifies and your light naturally shines upon your loved ones and the world.

If the story that you are now challenging has to do with abuse (sometimes this abuse can be a disease that is abusing you), it is very helpful to hold K2 jasper in your hand. Then enter into a meditative state and ask me to help you believe in your loving truth so that it is easy to rise above the unkind story of abuse.

Gabriel

I will heal your mental struggle by helping you recognize your own goodness. With this comes the healing of your soul, which leads to perfect happiness.

I am the angel of mental strength. I hear your prayers and I answer them by helping you discover your own goodness. When you recognize your goodness, your mind will be at peace. When the mind is at peace, the heart is at peace and all is healed.

Before working with me, please eat a piece of fruit. The fruit reminds you of you own sweetness. Then enter into a meditative state. I will sit with your energy for a while and help you see yourself as God sees, a perfect embodiment of the divine spirit. As you feel this perfection, a deep sense of forgiveness of yourself and others will penetrate you. From forgiveness, you will discover both your strength and your stillness. This healing will always lead to a deeper level of fulfillment and happiness. I am the love that is always with you. Amen.

Hadraniel

I awaken your memory of eternal love so that you discover your glorious life.

I am the angel who brings God's unconditional love to you. In my presence you can only feel love for yourself and others. In my presence you feel safe recognizing your own fears and negativity. In my presence, the recognition of your needed emotional healing is easy because you only feel love for human fragility and struggle (including your own). Once your needs are recognized, your newly found self-love penetrates every corner of your being and you are healed.

When working with me, I ask that you diffuse lime essential oil and breathe it in for a few minutes. Sit with me in silence and ask to feel God's love. Once you feel the love, ask to be shown the areas of grief, shame, embarrassment and guilt that require healing. I will send love to each of these pain points. Shame does not exist in the presence of love. Love truly heals all.

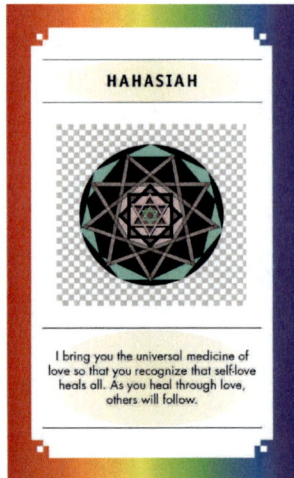

Hahasiah

I bring you the universal medicine of love so that you recognize that self-love heals all. As you heal through love, others will follow.

I am the angel of healers (both traditional and spiritual). I am able to help heal both diagnosable and mysterious illnesses. I help your healers find the answers they are looking for. In truth, healing always comes from self-love—either in the from of courageously fighting an illness or from digging through the emotional root of your pain to release the illness.

Please find light and dark colored pens or crayons and a piece of paper, then call me in. Get very still and then with the dark pen start to draw an image that represents your pain points that cause hate. (Try not to think before you start drawing.) You may feel a few aches and pains in your body as you draw. Then please use your light pen to draw light into your darkness. Repeat this exercise any time you have either physical or emotional aches and pains. (You may also visualize this exercise if you don't have the materials on hand.) The pain will either disappear or I will direct you to the solution.

Haniel

I will open the hearts of those in conflict to discover the pleasure that comes from support and love.

I am the angel of manifestation. I will help you release your inner conflicts and outer conflicts so that you know yourself fully. Once you actualize into authenticity, manifestation is a natural process. Conflicts block manifestation because your inner dialog is sending mixed messages to the universe. The result of releasing being confused by conflict is a happier and more fulfilling life.

To work with me, diffuse cinnamon and breathe it in for a few minutes. Enter into a meditative state and ask for your conflicts to surface so that I can see them. I will then guide your heart energy to resolve the internal and external conflicts by helping you see that both sides of the conflict are one and the same. Then I will take you to open doors (inside and outside of meditation). Walk through the doors with your head held high – the blended answer is on the other side.

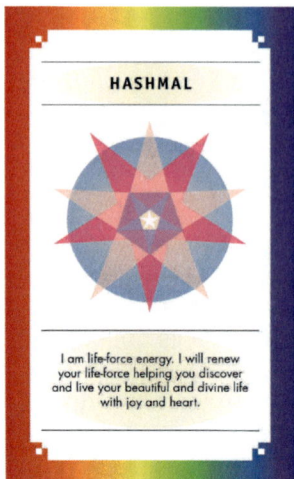

Hashmal

I am life-force energy. I will renew your life-force helping you discover and live your beautiful and divine life with joy and heart.

I am the angel of renewal. I am the energetic connection between you and all the love in the universe and beyond. When you connect to love, you are unstoppable.

To work with me, diffuse wild orange and breathe it in for a few minutes. Take a brief inventory of your life and acknowledge the areas that you would like to refresh and renew (family, friendships, romance, vocation, diet, exercise, spiritual practice, gratitude, health, service etc.) Once you decide on your focus for renewal I will guide you. Simply state: "I am ready to refresh and renew $_{areas}$. Please show me the way." You may enter a meditative state so that I can energetically direct you. You can also simply be aware that I am with you, sending you messages and opening doors so that you can take easy actions that lead to magnificent results. You are an unstoppable force of love and light.

Helet

I bring light when you are dark. I bring love when you are sad. I will lift your spirit so that you discover happiness.

I am the angel that is here to uplift you. It is so easy to feel despair. We experience devastating news stories and events and it somehow seems that the goodness in the world is gone. I am here to remind you that good and bad always seem to exist to provide contrast so that you can choose how you want to live. As you experience this contrast I am here to remind you that as you choose love, those around you will choose love too. And then all spirits are lifted and happy.

To work with me, diffuse ginger essential oil and breathe it in for a few minutes. Before you start meditation, I give you permission to gripe and complain about all that ails and concerns you. Then I ask that you take five deep breaths. Because of my presence during meditation, you will no longer be able to conjure up your concerns. Instead you will feel absolute peace. Within absolute peace you will remember that the world is still and always a beautiful place because in the end all is always love.

Imamiah

I am here to help you release your guilt and your mistakes and errors with ease. I am lifting your energy to your divine state of grace.

I am your guardian angel. I heal the human propensity to hold onto guilt, shame and embarrassment. I help you recover from you mistakes while renewing your mind, body, spirit and soul.

To work with me diffuse bergamot essential oil then breathe it in for a few minutes. Start your meditation with the affirmation, "I am a student of life. The more that I explore, the more that I live." During your meditation I ask that you share with me your mistakes and embarrassments and I will help you see the divine synchronicity of every moment of your life. I will help your mind reframe itself to acknowledge your life's perfection. You will now naturally feel grace for all that you have done and all that you are. Now you are an unstoppable force of love and light.

Jarahmeel

I see how sad you feel at times but I also see your beautiful light. I will help you see and feel your light and shine with the stars.

I am the angel of prophetic visions. I see beyond your day-to-day human existence and recognize your divine plan. I help you release the illness and emotional pain distracting you from embracing your star-potential.

To work with me, hold an azurite crystal.[4] Then state: "I am very grateful for my beautiful gifts. I have the courage to use them fully. I know that I will be safe and protected as I do. We are blessed." Breathe deeply and ask me to join you in meditation. I will help you clear your mind so that you can see how blessed your world will be when you shine your light. I will release your stressors so that choosing to shine is easy because you fully desire to be a blessing onto the world as the world blesses you. We are healed.

---

[4] If azurite is not available hold any quartz crystal.

Jehudiel

I am the angel of light workers. I am guiding you to share your light with the world. I am energizing your purpose and spirit so that your work brings bliss.

Sometimes it feels difficult to be a light worker when there are no answers for why atrocities happen. It is not for a light worker to understand all. Instead, a light worker stays in a place of love even if it seems that the world has gone dark. When you remain in love, then the darkness dissipates faster, simply because you are love. Then you are surrounded by a loving community that shows the world that in our hearts there is no place for hate and atrocities.

When you work with me, please diffuse wintergreen essential oil and breathe it in for a few minutes. Then enter into a meditative state by asking God (or the universe) how you can serve. Your fears may surface. Then I will help dissolve your fears and distrust of humankind by surrounding your heart with light. When you are fearless, no one else can have fear. And then the world is healed.

Jophiel

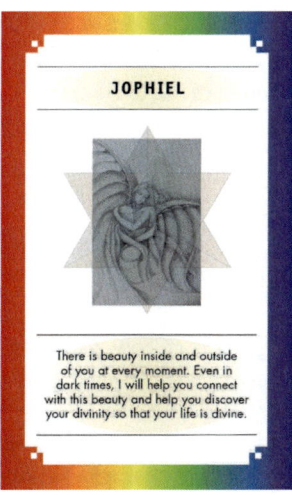

There is beauty inside and outside of you at every moment. Even in dark times, I will help you connect with this beauty and help you discover your divinity so that your life is divine.

I am the guardian of Torah[5] and of wisdom itself. As the guardian of Torah, I also energize the mystical tradition of Kabbalah. My name is translated as "of beauty". When there is hate, I help all find their beauty through study, wisdom and mysticism. One cannot always understand hate, but we can always use moments of hate to turn to love and bring the communities of the world together.

When you have experienced something dark, I ask you to diffuse frankincense essential oil and breathe it in. Then I will join you in your meditation. I will give you the loving guidance that will help you create beauty from the dark. If desired, I will lead you to mystical studies that can help you make sense of a world that appears ugly. And eventually, I will help you discover the love that is always there, in every situation, always.

---

[5] Hebrew Bible (Old Testament)

Kerubiel

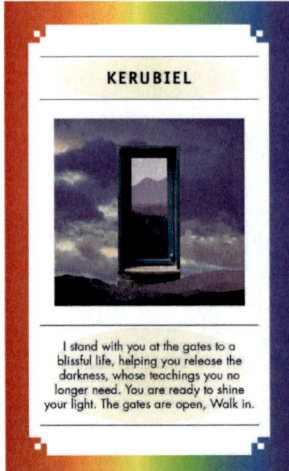

I stand with you at the gates to a blissful life, helping you release the darkness, whose teachings you no longer need. You are ready to shine your light. The gates are open, Walk in.

I am the prince of the gates of Heaven and everlasting open doors. I stand at the portal to all planes and dimensions. When you are ready to experience deeper and deeper awareness of love, I will help you expand into a multidimensional consciousness so that you can experience Heaven on Earth. My being expands into the depths of all existence.

To ready yourself for the experience of Heaven on Earth, I ask that you first diffuse lemon essential oil and breathe in the oil for a few minutes. Then begin your meditation by asking to be shown that which gives you fear and then repeat, "I replace fear with love." (I will be in your presence as you do this so that the fear will not feel daunting.) Repeat this practice until fearful states have dissipated. As they dissipate, your life will become fuller, richer and more loving. I will open the multidimensional portal at the speed that you are ready.

Laileh

I come from the night and turn dark into light. I am birth and rebirth. I will turn your darkness into light.

I am the angel of transformation. The start of the transformation comes for the churning, burning and yearning that rises in the dark of the night. I will use your unsettledness to help you discover your calling. I will give you the courage to follow your calling and your rebirth follows. I am all that is and all that can be. I am the angel of transformation.

Call on me during the night when you are churning, burning and yearning. Still yourself for a few minutes and I will merge with you. I will gather your restlessness and create a passionate fire in you to follow the call to service and change. I will send you visions so that you can see how courageous change will bring you back to life. Your journey will be a heroic one, bringing you peace, love and bliss.

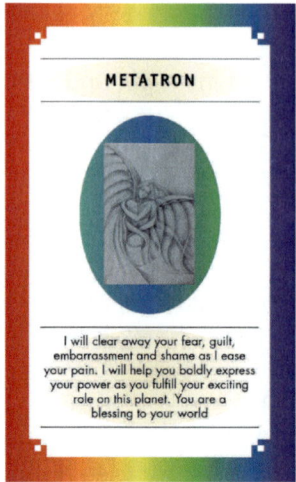

Metatron

I will clear away your fear, guilt, embarrassment and shame as I ease your pain. I will help you boldly express your power as you fulfill your exciting role on this planet. You are a blessing to your world

I am the celestial scribe. I translate God's words into books through earthly channels. I also deliver symbols through these channels, which are the keys to understanding mystical realties. The sole purpose of bringing you God's words is to help you choose to release your shame, and perception of sin, then willingly empower yourself to use your gifts to be a blessing onto the world.

To work with me, stare at the symbol below for a few minutes thereby entering into a meditative state. Once in meditation I will answer the universal question of how to be fulfilled and happy. You will hear words and see symbols and images. If you repeat this exercise for a few days, you will gain the courage and knowingness that you require to proceed on your enlightened journey to fulfillment and success.

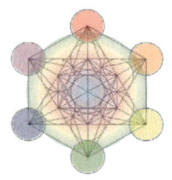

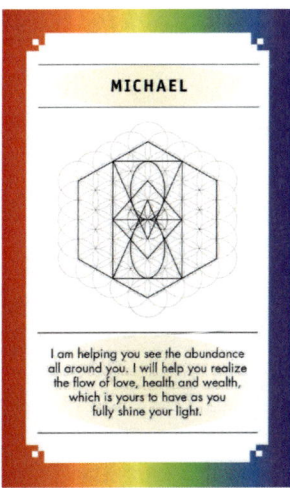

Michael

I am helping you see the abundance all around you. I will help you realize the flow of love, health and wealth, which is yours to have as you fully shine your light.

I am the angel that will lead you to discover that you are the light of God. When this fact is no longer in question, then all the bounty of the earth is yours to have.

To work with me diffuse oregano essential oil and breathe it in for a few minutes. Then enter a meditative state. Ask me to help you experience so much love that you are in communion with God. When in communion, you become God and all of your pain and suffering lifts. In oneness with God, you are then able to lift the pain and suffering of others. The world is bountiful. The world is healed. Amen.

Muriel

There is no need for fear my beloved one. I will help you release your pain as you discover the pleasure that is yours to have. Your life is a blessing.

I am the angel that will open your heart. Opening the heart can be scary as you are afraid that vulnerability leads to pain. My special connection with pets and plants helps me help you find peace by connecting with energies of unconditional love (such as your dog).

To work with me I ask that you diffuse peppermint and visualize drawing this sacred essence into all the pores of you body. Then visualize the peppermint surrounding your heart. At this point show me the energy that you are not able to be unconditionally loving towards. You may see a swirl of peppermint oil surrounding this image. Then I will help you open your heart to this energy and you will experience your fear softening and your love growing. If we work together daily, you fear dissipates and your heart will grow. All is healed with unconditional love.

Netzach

I am helping you create your world of sublime beauty. It is beautiful to be alive at this time and you are a blessing.

I am the angel of eternity. When the fear of death is removed from life (because in truth this is no death), there is no fear and everything is beautiful. Without fear, you will feel free to spread your wings and fly.

To work with me, diffuse geranium essential oil and breathe it in for a few minutes. Enter into a meditative state and I will show you images of what eternity looks like here on earth. While you receive these images your fears will dissipate. Your understanding of heaven on earth will take form and you will recognize the beauty that is always there when there is no fear. You life is truly a blessing.

Note: The Beauty Grid from **Divine Grids a Celebration of Crystal Healing** *by Rebecca Cohen is energetically opened to support this meditation and healing. If you have the book, it is recommended to build the grid and have it present during this meditation.*

Nithael

I am here to enlighten your energy to its natural state of youthfulness. I am helping you release your stressors and pain so that you can enjoy every day with ease.

I am your healer angel. When you work with me, I will rejuvenate you and help you discover your inner child. My specialty is returning your mind to a healthy and happy place. I am also the healer's healer. With my help, you will discover the natural ways to nurture yourself so that you find it easy to fulfill your calling to help others. In other words, I am the angel of self-care.

To work with me, I ask that you diffuse and breathe in ginger for a few minutes. Then enter into a meditative state. In meditation, share your thoughts and fears with me. I will receive those thoughts (so you can release them) and send you visions of the revitalized future that is yours to have. As you continue this meditative practice it will be harder to conjure up the negativity and the positive images will be commonplace. The more your mind sees the positive the more happy your physical reality will be.

Nuriel

I connect you to your passionate fire so that you discover your voice and live your richly fulfilling dreams.

I am the angel of passion. You have extinguished your passionate flame because passion makes you vulnerable to criticism. It's not easy to extinguish the flame, so you unconsciously do so by allowing dis-ease to enter your mind, body, spirit and soul. I will help you rise above the criticism by helping you discover how glorious the reconnection is.

I ask that you list all the activities that you feel passionate about. Then consider your list and ask yourself why you don't make time for these activities. You may believe that your passions are useless, expensive, irresponsible or impossible for other reasons, I will help you recognize that your excuses are just the fear that you aren't good enough or that your desires will be misunderstood and criticized. I ask that you imagine yourself doing each activity. I will show you the splendor that surrounds you as you engage. I will help you release your fears knowing that your passions are your divine gifts and the key to your fulfillment and happiness.

Peniel

I will help you find hope during hard times. There is always hope because there is always love and love is always the answer.

I am the angel of divine solutions. The solution is to find a little more love and forgiveness in your heart every day. This extra love leads to the desire to serve. While serving, you will always find hope because you have discovered the best part of self. With this discovery, you love a little more and the upward spiral grows.

To work with me, visual   arting at the outside of the spiral and moving towards the center. At the center, fill your cup up with self-love. Then move back along the spiral to the outside; at the end-point visualize yourself serving others. Then repeat this exercise until serving yourself and serving others feel like the same thing.

Raguel

I am your friend. I will always listen. You will hear my voice responding with compassion as I help you find your answers. I am here, always.

I am the angel of justice. When you feel that things are unfair, which leads you to despair, I will help you find peace. Life is sometimes a puzzle, but the pieces can always be put together so that we see the road to move towards fulfillment and happiness.

To work with me I ask that you diffuse melaleuca and breathe it in for a few minutes. Then enter a meditative state. In this state, ask me your questions and share with me your sorrows and feelings of injustice. I will listen compassionately then show you the pieces of the puzzle that can help you make sense of your life. You will feel the puzzle completing itself and as you do, you will feel peace, calm and understanding. Your life is whole.

Raphael

I bring you the experience of absolute self-love, which helps you release guilt and embarrassment. Without these difficult emotions, your body, mind and spirit will harmonize to perfect health.

I am God's healer. Hand me your problems and I will help you resolve them. Your disease is your mask to hide your embarrassment, which is always related to guilt. I will help you see that exploring, then releasing, your hidden feelings is a much healthier way to live than wearing your painful mask.

To work with me, diffuse frankincense essential oil and breathe it in for a few minutes. I ask you to tell me what embarrasses you most about a loved one. Then I will help you turn this concept around so that you discover how you are actually embarrassed about yourself for the same reason. I will help you recognize the guilt under the embarrassment. It always relates to one of these hidden emotional states:
- I am unappealing
- I am greedy
- I am foolish
- I am irresponsible or lazy

Then I will help you release the identified embarrassment and guilt through compassionate self-love, knowing that when you do, your health will improve.

Raziel

I am with you as you explore your soul's secrets. Sharing those secrets is safe and will heal you. With my guidance, you will know absolute love.

I unlock mysteries. I will open up your psychic vision, past life exploration, connections through numerology, recognition of signs and synchronicities and here-to-fore non-identified ways of exploring your soul. To journey with me is one of intrigue and excitement. The end result is that when guided by me, you find it fascinating to reach deeper and deeper as clear your soul of its layers of pain.

To work with me I ask that you diffuse helichrysum and breathe it in for a few minutes. As you enter a meditative state, I will show you symbols, such as an infinity. These symbols unlock the mysteries held by your soul in other planes and dimensions. Then ask me a specific question such as: Why I am hurting? To answer, I may reveal a past life, a new healing technique to explore, or direct you to healing through **The Path to Heal** sessions, which is the solving the mystery lover's modality.

Remiel

I am the angel of your future. I am sending you visions so that you can see that your future is so beautiful that you decide to step in to it now.

I am the angel of hope. I help you see the world as it really is--a magical playground wherein only love is real. I help you understand that pain is an illusion because in truth, you are a spiritual being living in a physical form. As you recognize that pain only exists to teach you to know love and compassion for yourself and others, you discover how quickly pain dissolves.

To receive my help, I ask that you diffuse lemon essential oil and breathe it in. Enter into a meditative state and share with me the bleakness that is overtaking you. Then breathe gently and I will send you visions of your wondrous future. Repeat this exercise daily until the bleakness in your life is replaced by wondrous and compassionate amazement.

Rikbiel

I am the angel of the merkaba, the holy chariot. I will guide you on your multi-dimensional journey through all the planes and dimensions of your soul's existence to release pain and discover happiness.

When you journey with me, you discover that all pain is held to help us learn something and grow. That something is always to discover deeper and deeper love for self and others. By leading you on this multi-dimensional journey through your soul's layers, I am able to expedite growth by leading you to hidden fears that are holding you back and then giving you the courage to choose love.

To work with me, hold a merkaba crystal or stare at the merkaba on this card. Take a few deep breaths and enter a meditative state. As fears pop into your head through mental chatter, I will facilitate the subtle understanding that the fear can be released by choosing love, and I will help you make that choice. When all fear is gone, there is only love.

Author's note: Since channeling in this exercise from Rikbiel, when I find myself in mental chatter, in my mind's eye, I see a merkaba pinging through my head like a ping pong ball and the chatter clears.

Sachiel

I am here to remind you that you are fully supported by the universe when you pursue endeavors that fill you with passion. I will help you take the risk to follow your heart.

I am the angel of expansion. I expand your heart and your wealth as you follow your dreams. I will also expand your vision so that passion takes you to places beyond imagination.

To work with me diffuse lemon essential oil and breathe it in for a few minutes. Then enter a meditative state and share with me what excites you. Then you will experience you presence growing as your vibration raises higher. You will recognize what your limitless pure potential feels like. After experiencing your potential in meditation it will be easy for you to actualize as your expanded self in your physical reality.

Salaphiel

I hear all of your prayers and the prayers of your loved ones. I will lead you to the easy answers that will ease your pain and help you discover your greatness. I am the love that is always with you.

I am the love of God. I listen to all of your hopes, dreams and requests for help. When you work with me, I provide you focus, blocking out distractions, so that you hear the wisdom that surrounds you. You now receive the guidance that you are asking for. Once you have perfected the art of listening, I help you go deeper into your soul to discover what it is you are looking for.

When working with me, I ask that you diffuse clary sage essential oil and breathe it in for a few minutes. Then enter a meditative state. In this state please ask, pray and express. I will help you gain focus so that both inside and outside of meditation, you will receive your answers. Inside our practice, you will naturally start to know and trust yourself and therefore you will reveal your deepest hopes and dreams to us your angels. It is through the focused asking and listening that you will become a walking being of manifestation and your life will be synchronistic ease.

Sandalphon

While you explore your soul for healing, I will protect your being and the earth.

I specialize in helping those that are trapped in fear and negativity. My closeness to the earth helps me recognize lower vibrational energy and give you the courage to transmute this energy to the highest vibration of all, the vibration of unconditional love. From this space, your creative soul will awaken. From your pain, you will create love, and then from love, you will expand into greater and greater love. You will feel the connectedness of all the energy of the earth and you will vibrate with possibility and potential. You will be a blessing to all those that you meet.

To work with me, please diffuse wild orange essential oil and breathe it in for a few minutes. Then please enter a meditative state and share your fears with me. As you share them, a matrix will appear in your psychic vision. This matrix will connect you to every other earthly soul. Then I will send love to your fear. That love will travel through the matrix and touch every human. Outside of meditation you will recognize every soul as one that you already know. When you are in their presence they will feel the love that you already shared with them. Your connection will be divine. You will feel at home anywhere and everywhere and therefore you will easily share your gifts. We are united and blessed.

Sarah

I am always with you, removing fear from your liver so that you flow only with the energy of the heart. Your fear is gone; there is only love.

I am the angel of motherly love. I exist inside of you so that you are always nurtured by the unconditional love of a loving mother. Because I am inside of you, whatever your external circumstances are, you always feel love. In this state of love, it is natural to release the darkest fears that you may carry.

To work with me, please take three deep breaths and then diffuse lavender essential oil. Then place a hand on your heart and enter a meditative state. While you stay very still in mind and body, I will flow to your fear and fill your liver with light to dissolve the fear. Your mind does not need to be actively thinking of anything as I do my work. You will know when it is time to finish the meditation, but I will continue my loving work even as you go about your day. Enjoy the lightness that replaces the fear.

Seraphina

I am here to enhance the open and loving communication between you and your loved ones. I will help you experience your family's love even if your family has forgotten that only love is real.

I am the angel of family harmony. The only reason that family can be disharmonious is to push each other to grow into deeper love by overcoming the adversarial qualities of the relationships.

To work with me, diffuse clary sage essential oil and breathe it in for a few minutes. Then enter into a meditative state and visualize the first loved one that is giving you pain. Then ask this love one: "Why are we in pain?" The answer will always be some form of "to teach you unconditional self-love." I will send love to your "rejected aspects of self" until there is only love. (I will then send the love through your genetic line so that these rejected aspects are now loved by all.) Repeat this step for each loved one with whom there is a painful issue. The meditation is over when the painful images transmute to loving symbols and feelings. This meditation should be repeated daily until love is the primary energy between you and all of your loved ones. And then you know the truth, that only love is real.

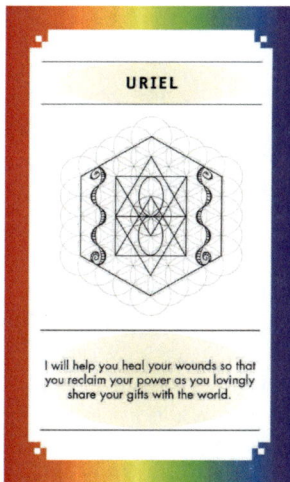

Uriel

I will help you heal your wounds so that you reclaim your power as you lovingly share your gifts with the world.

I am the angel of The Shift. I am guiding you through your healing so that you actualize into peace, love and prosperity. As your transformation unfolds, others shift around you, and the world is enlightened.

To work with me, hold a labrodorite crystal and take three deep breaths. Then enter into a meditative state by repeating the mantra, "I Am That I Am." I will remind you during your meditation that you are: peace, love, prosperity, fulfilled, joy and bliss. I am letting you know that you are already enlightened. This meditation helps you release your blocks and negativities so that you reclaim your power. I Am That I Am.

Uzziel

I am here to release you from that which is no longer serving you. I am helping you gladly give up that which is not of love.

I am the angel of strength, which comes from faith. Faith is the knowingness that you are on a divine path and that that path is always love regardless of circumstance. With the strength of faith, it is easy to make the changes that bring greater and greater happiness and fulfillment.

Start your meditation by viewing the portal above. While looking at the portal ask me to help you recognize that which isn't serving you. Then visualize cutting the cords to these stressors. If you do this exercise frequently, you will easily find your strength to cut the cords through decisive change. I help you discover the faith that changes made from love always bring greater happiness.

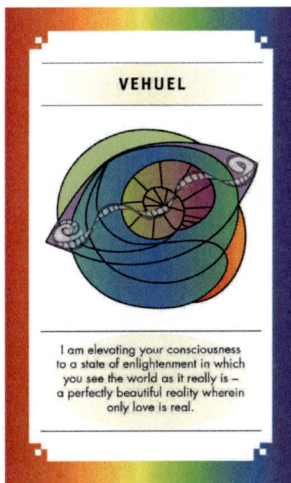

Vehuel

I am elevating your consciousness to a state of enlightenment in which you see the world as it really is – a perfectly beautiful reality wherein only love is real.

I am the angel of elevation. I will elevate your consciousness to higher levels of love. To do this I must remove all shame, which originated from this lifetime or prior lifetime conditioning.

To work with me, please diffuse bergamot essential oil and breathe it in for a few minutes. Enter a meditative state. I ask that you let me see the origin of your shame. It may be from this lifetime or a prior lifetime. When you share this memory with me, I will pour unconditional love into your soul. This memory is now transmuted to love and you will feel lighter and free.

Note: The Transcendence Grid from **Divine Grids a Celebration of Crystal Healing** *by Rebecca Cohen is energetically opened to support this meditation and healing. If you have the book, it is recommended to build the grid and have it present during this meditation.*

Zadkiel

When you are in the presence of suffering, I will help you feel only compassion. This will ease the suffering for all.

I am the angel of freedom. I free your mind from anger and fear, which frees you from suffering. What is left is compassion.

To work with me diffuse spearmint essential oil and breathe it in for a few minutes. Then take a quick inventory of all the suffering that directly impacts you. Ask me to help you send love to the suffering. As you send love, your fear and anger dissipate and your compassion increases. While continuing this practice, it becomes harder to feel anything but love because in truth, only love is real. The end state is peace and peace is freedom.

Zaphkiel

I am here to inspire you to be completely compassionate to yourself. This will allow you to use your talents to their fullest. I will open your brainwaves to your brilliance. I am your magic.

I am the angel that brings you the knowledge of God. The key to communing with the God that surrounds you, is to discover the God within you. This discovery occurs when you are completely compassionate to yourself. Compassion makes you unstoppable. Your gifts, talents and brilliance are allowed to shine.

To work with me please diffuse ylang ylang and breathe it in for a few minutes. Enter a meditative state. I ask that you allow me to see all of your guilt and shame. I will shower you with love while doing so, so that you discover compassion for yourself. This compassion will lead to complete forgiveness of self and others. Your vibration is now raised to love. It will now be easy for you to discover your gifts, talents and brilliance. You will discover the magic that your life becomes when you have only love for yourself and others.

*Note: The Miracle of Me Grid from **Divine Grids a Celebration of Crystal Healing** by Rebecca Cohen is energetically opened to support this meditation and healing. If you have the book, it is recommended to build the grid and have it present during this meditation.*

Path Practitioner Protocols

Protocol: Perfectly Imperfect

1) It is my true desire to actualize into the true me. However, I am afraid that I am not deserving because I'm not sure that I am forgivable [for $_{subject}$.]

   Therefore I hold back through:

   ❖ demanding my own and other's perfection
   ❖ a lack of forgiveness for weakness
   ❖ holding all (including myself) to a high standard
   ❖ pretending to maintain perfect control
   ❖ feeling alienated
   ❖ over-accommodating
   ❖ being overwhelmed by stressors
   ❖ holding onto other's truths rather than my own (family fundamentalism)

	Nuummite 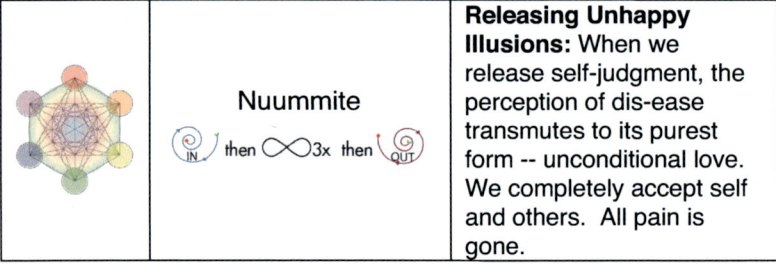	Releasing Unhappy Illusions: When we release self-judgment, the perception of dis-ease transmutes to its purest form -- unconditional love. We completely accept self and others. All pain is gone.

2) Pick a **Path** Angel Card or dowse TOC to determine angel to help us remember that our perfect imperfections are in fact perfect and to help us fulfill our dreams.

Protocol: Family Love

1) I have not been able to break away from _{love-one(s)}'s fundamental belief that _{life affirming activity(s)/duality word(s)/ basic need(s)} causes pain.

2) I release this belief because I now know that only love is real so I choose to love myself and therefore I have the space to love everything.

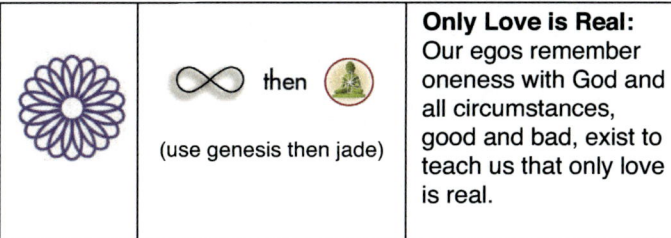

		Only Love is Real: Our egos remember oneness with God and all circumstances, good and bad, exist to teach us that only love is real.
	(use genesis then jade)	

3) Pick a **Path** Angel card Dowse TOC to go see which angel can help us release the illusion of pain that we hold onto so as to hold back with our families rather than fly.

Protocol: Sacred Truths

1) Dowse which Sacred Truths are conflicting with Family Fundamentalism (see Intro for definition). For each conflict:
   a. Pick a **Path** angel card(s) to gain insight and align the family to truth
   b. Dowse to go to same angel in this book to dig deeper
   c. Repeat for all truths out of alignment

Sacred Truths
1) All humans have the same biology.
2) All souls are equal, perfect and fully connected to each other.
3) Genes contain both spiritual and biological information.
4) Giving and receiving always balance because they are one and the same thing.
5) Human evolution will lead to peace, love and oneness.
6) I am the world. My truths and untruths are reflected by everyone and everything.
7) Illness or discomfort is a label that simply illuminates what the body, mind and spirit need to heal.
8) Living in joy means appreciating that life is what happens while you're busy making other plans.
9) Peace begins with me and no one else.
10) Peace comes from loving thy neighbor as thyself.
11) Self-love is the only path to heal.
12) The plant and animal world are fully connected to our energetic being.
13) All our problems can be solved if we get in touch with, and follow, our hearts.
14) When I have no fear, no one in my presence can fear.
15) When I am complete faith, my life is miraculous.
16) When in alignment with my authentic self, my true desires naturally manifest.

2)

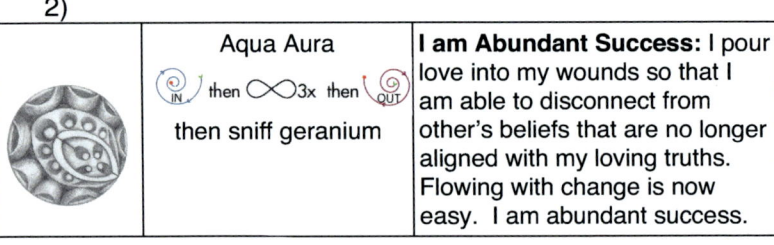

	Aqua Aura (IN) then ∞3x then (OUT) then sniff geranium	**I am Abundant Success:** I pour love into my wounds so that I am able to disconnect from other's beliefs that are no longer aligned with my loving truths. Flowing with change is now easy. I am abundant success.

Protocol: I Shine

1) I release _{illuminating condition(s)}, which had been blocking my full potential, because I'm no longer afraid of _{subject}'s _{duality word(s)/emotion(s)} that my full potential may surface.

	3 crystal ring
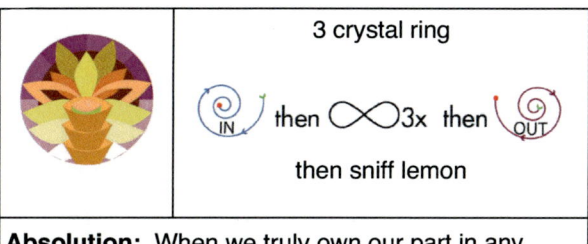	then ∞3x then then sniff lemon
Absolution: When we truly own our part in any conflict, the guilt may feel overwhelming. However, it is at that moment of reckoning that we are showered with divine love, which will dissolve the guilt because in the end, only love is real.	

2) Pick **Path** angel card or dowse TOC to help us release our fears that are holding us back.

55

Card Spreads

For each spread, pick cards from **The Embraced By Your Angels Deck** associated with the ovals on each page. Feel free to get more insight from the same angel's message in this book.

I Fill My Life with Peace

1. Restful Sleep
2. Life Affirming Work
3. Loving Relationships
4. Peaceful Home
5. Healthy Body
6. Enlightened Heart

Conflict Resolution

- Identify the person or subject you are conflict with
- Then pick 2 sets of cards, one for you and one for the conflicted subject for each of following subjects:

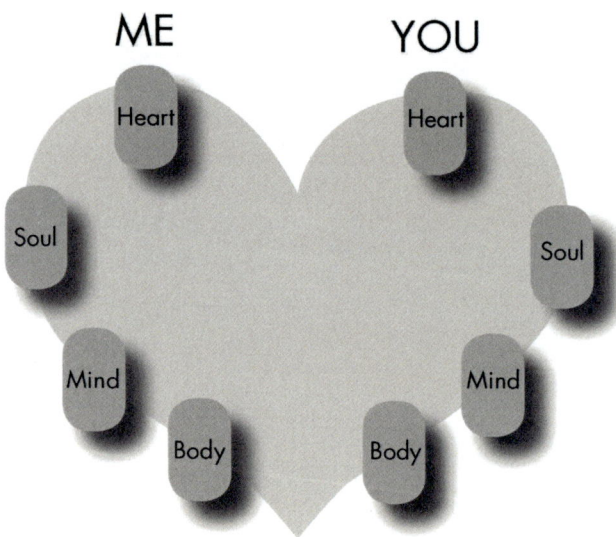

Chronic Illness

I empower myself to heal:
1. mind
2. body
3. spirit
4. soul

which results in perfect health

Books By Rebecca Cohen

Mystical Manifestation – Learn Divine Magic, a manifestation tool that accelerates the fulfillment of your dreams.

Divine Grids: a Celebration of Crystal Healing – Included are 80 pre-formed crystal grid diagrams designed to help overcome specific lifelong struggles.

What My Dog is Teaching Me About Me: Dog Training the Easy Way – This book decodes how your dog's unwanted behavior is mirroring your deepest fears. This book will help you resolve those fears, thereby resolving the behavioral issues as well.

Only Love is Real: a Book of Inspirational Verse (art by Shiya Stone)

Angelic Blessings – Essential oil based blended remedies channeled from your angels to heal the mind, body, spirit and soul.

I Have No Fear, There is No Pain (with Barbra Burleigh) – A series of vignettes that describe how, on a very unconscious level, we often hold onto dis-ease because we are altruistic beings and have the belief that our dis-ease is somehow helping another. Included for each area of dis-ease is a Prescription for Joy,

My Path to Joy (with Lisa Orlandi) – A series of **Path** protocols that provide insight to help you remove your blocks to joy.

We Are The Shift – I asked the angels a series of questions about stubborn issues. Through these channeled answers, we are guided to the meaning of these issues and how releasing them will lead the planet's vibrational shift into unconditional love.

Seasons of Love -- The energies of the planet shift with the changing seasons and the changing tides. The essential oil recipes for healing contained within change based on the season, the Zodiac month, and the time of day. These recipes, diffused into the atmosphere, restore our natural state of infinite grace.

Discovering Enlightenment in the Age of Donald Trump – This Q&A with the angels shows us the way to bring peace to the divided world.

Soul Crystal Formations – These geometric crystal formations heal the depressed spirit by shifting unproductive energy to love. Formations usually require approximately 10 small pieces of the same crystal type. These formations call in all divine feminine energy to create enlightened and miraculous shifts.

Divine Consciousness -- A series of chakra opening exercises connecting us to our divine power and miraculously enlightening the mind, body, spirit and soul.

Plant Medicine, An Integrative Approach to Essential Oil Use -- A simple approach, delivering focused information on how to provide healing for the mind, body and spirit using specific essential oils.

Sound Medicine, Planetary Sound Healing for the New Age – A guide to using tuning fork vibration to tune our body, mind and spirit to our divine vibration. In divine vibration we are healthy, happy, loving and following our path.

Crystal Medicine for the New Age – A guide to using the beauty of crystal energy to transmute unhealthy crystalized body and mind formations to the body's natural state of perfect health and unconditional love.

Food Love Medicine – A guide to using the spiritual properties of food to enrich our lives. Natural foods contain all the goodness we need to heal mind, body, spirit and soul.

Meditate with Your Angels – This book is both a guide book to accompany the **Embraced By Your Angels** card deck and a stand-alone book which leads you through a meditative practice with your angels.

Card Decks – by Rebecca Cohen

The Path to Heal Card Decks (eight decks)
available only at www.thepathtoheal.com

The five miracle decks are: Peace, Blessings, Ease, Love and Abundance. Each contains 44 healing cards with beautiful images and affirmations.

The two specialty decks are: Embraced By Your Angels (Biblical angels card deck) and Divine Consciousness (enlightenment deck).

The two loving tarot cards and guide books are: Doggie Love Tarot, Mystical Kitten Tarot.

Made in the USA
Middletown, DE
28 April 2019